Teashops

in the
LAKE DISTRICT

Teashop Walks

in the
LAKE DISTRICT

Ron Freethy

COUNTRYSIDE BOOKS
NEWBURY, BERKSHIRE

Contents

Walk

Introduction

As a child brought up in the Lake District in the 1940s and 1950s, my birthday treat was always a train journey to the steamer pier at Lakeside. Then it was onto the boats – either the Teal or the Swan – to Ambleside and, from there, would be an enjoyable walk along the shores of the lake. No trip was complete without a visit to a café.

This is a fascination which has been with me ever since, and my son and now my grandson have been my companions on many of my teashop walks. The lakeside trip has changed little over time, since steam trains still ply between Haverthwaite and Lakeside, and a steamer service operates throughout the year. Also, it is now possible to combine a walk with a ferry trip based on Ullswater and this is a service which, from 2005, operates throughout the year.

All of my favourite walks included in this book begin close to teashops overlooking either rivers as at Grasmere and Pooley Bridge or lakes as at Keswick and Bassenthwaite. There are also coastal walks where it is sensible to begin and end at a teashop and there are lovely meanderings at Maryport and undulations at Ulverston, Coniston and Waterhead at Ambleside.

These 20 walks will also appeal to the historian with Roman remains at Ambleside, Maryport and especially Hadrian's Wall at Birdoswald, the Norse cross at Gosforth, and the Iron Age fort above Pooley Bridge. Then there is one of the best preserved Augustinian priories to be found in England, which dominates the village of Cartmel. There are also very enjoyable and leisurely strolls through literature with the Tennyson connection at Bassenthwaite and of course the Wordsworths at Grasmere.

Sketch maps are included for each walk, with numbered points that correspond with the numbered paragraphs in the text, but it is wise to carry with you the relevant Ordnance Survey Explorer map, details of which are provided. Suggestions of where to park are given, but do always obtain the proprietor's permission if you wish to leave your car in the car park of a teashop or café. And, please use common sense wherever you park, and do not obstruct entrances or private parking places.

The walks vary in length between 2½ and 7 miles. As such they have been designed with families in mind or those who, like me, want to stop and admire the view as they follow well-marked routes. I hope readers will enjoy these treks and teashops as much as I have during the preparation of this book.

Ron Freethy

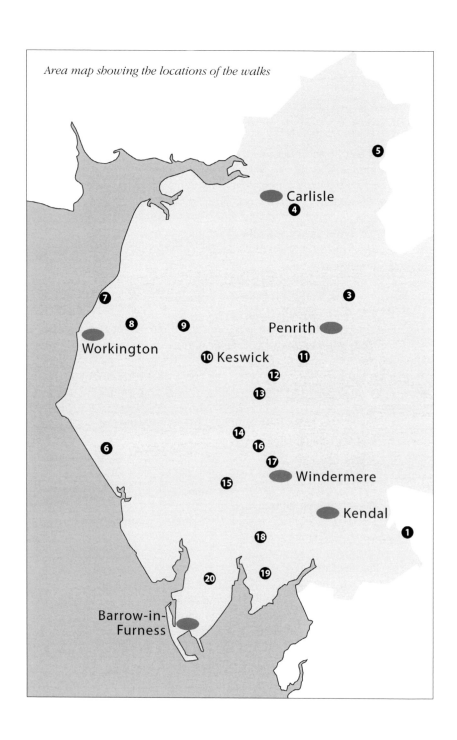

Area map showing the locations of the walks

Walk 1
DENT

This gently undulating walk is based around one of Britain's most attractive and unspoiled villages. From Dent's historic church the route follows the River Dee as it meanders beneath small but majestic bridges and is overlooked by moorlands and mountains. Wildlife abounds and visitors from near and far take their time to study an area famous for its geological formations. The stroll passes old cottages, barns and farmhouses and through delightful rural landscapes.

The Rise Hill Kitchen overlooks the church. This pleasant little café serves all day breakfasts but the Wensleydale ploughman's lunch is a favourite with walkers especially as it can be purchased in a handy picnic pack. The soup is just what is advertised – home-made – and on a cool day this, and the toasted sandwiches, are most welcome. In hot weather the tables outside are well used and the milk shakes are worth the visit as are the homemade cakes. Teashops should always provide a good brew and this certainly applies to Rise Hill. It is open daily from 10 am to 5 pm. Telephone 015396 25209.

9

DISTANCE: 5 miles
TIME: Allow 2½ hours
MAP: OS Explorer OL2
STARTING POINT: The Pay & Display car park in Dent (GR 703869).
HOW TO GET THERE: Most visitors approach Dent from Sedburgh via a minor road off the A684 but there is access from Ingleton (which is on the A65) or from the A684 at Garsdale Head. Visitors should not be fooled by attempting to arrive via the Settle to Carlisle railway. Dent station is more than 4 miles from the village including a 1 in 3 incline! Next to the car park is a bus shelter complete with a tap and a brush where visitors can wash the mud off their boots at the conclusion of a stroll.

THE WALK

☕ **1.** From the car park turn left into Dent town, which is not so much a town as a small village but was named long ago when it was quite rightly regarded as the 'capital' of Dentdale. This is made up of a wonderful cluster of hamlets and isolated farms.

Continue along the narrow cobbled street, lined with old inns and quaint cottages.

Dent was famous for its knitters and some of the cottage windows were designed to make the maximum use of daylight. On the left there is a granite slab into which is built a fountain. This is a memorial to the Dent scientist Adam Sedgwick (1785–1873). This really was a case of a local lad made good because he became Professor of Geology at Cambridge and has long been regarded as the father of British geology. No doubt he was inspired by the local scenery.

From the fountain turn sharp left to enter the church of St Andrew.

This church dates to around 1080 and inside is some Norman stonework and with some magnificent box pews dating to the 17th century. Take time to visit the church and be sure to look carefully at the floor of the chancel. The polished marble reveals lots of fascinating fossils proving that the area around Dent was once covered by a shallow warm sea full of sea creatures with wonderfully shaped shells. Nearby is the old Grammar School, now a private residence.

From the church exit, look to the right to see the Rise Hill Kitchen Tea Shop. Turn left and descend a set of steps and then turn left to reach

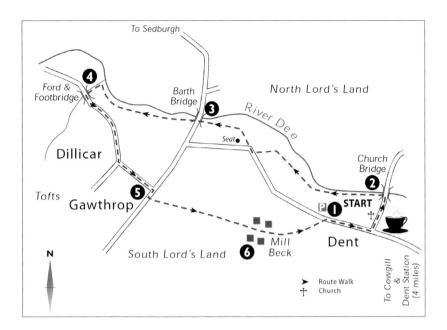

Church Bridge over the River Dee.

2. Do not cross the bridge but look for a narrow stile and a signpost leading left and signed Barth Bridge (1 mile). To the left over the fields are splendid views of the church. Cross a footbridge over a feeder stream leading down to the Dee but always keep the main river to the right. The path eases gently left and passes through a series of dog-friendly stiles. Approach a large metal gate after just over ½ mile. Turn left and then sharp right along a minor road. In less than 100 yards, there is a seat and another metal gate to the right. Pass through this gate and follow an obvious field path through a number of well maintained gates and stiles.

The route then bears left away from the river Dee, which is still on the right. Pass through a metal gate and a tiny footbridge and approach Barth Bridge.

The area to the right of the river is called North Lord's Land whilst the fertile fields to the left are called South Lord's Land.

3. Barth Bridge is reached via a substantial set of wooden steps. Do not cross this bridge but pass over a minor road where there is a sign indicating Ellers (1 mile) straight ahead. Ellers means the land by the water which is

The Sedgwick memorial with Dent church in the background.

a very accurate description. Descend another flight of wooden steps to the riverbank and the Dee is still on the right.

To the left is the impressive bulk of Combe Scar which is a long established grouse moor and also the site of old quarries with rock formations which were once the study area of Adam Sedgwick.

4. Approach a lane which is used by a farm called Dillicar. Continue along this and look for a footbridge and a ford over the tributary of the Dee. Turn left here and cross a stile. Bear right to Bower Bank and visible straight ahead and high above is the massive Whernside.

At 2,419 feet (737 metres), this is the highest of the three peaks and its height easily qualifies it to be considered as a mountain. The old name was actually Quernside, meaning a millstone area, and as the uplands are composed of millstone grit this makes good sense.

5. The obvious footpath soon becomes a more substantial track and leads into the atmospheric little hamlet of Gawthrop.

In the middle distance but not on this walk is an even smaller settlement called Toft – this is Danish and means brother. Gawthrop is a Celtic surname which later became Gough.

At Gawthrop, cross a bridge and at a T-junction turn right to Mill Beck.

The word beck is Scandinavian for a small stream. This particular beck once powered a mill but all traces of this have now gone. Mill Beck farm, however, is an attractive spot with lots of well-drained fields leading down to the river Dee. The site has recently been developed into a splendid little campsite which is very popular with families. Although it is small, Dent still has a good number of inexpensive bed and breakfast establishments.

6. From Mill Beck follow an obvious track for about ¼ mile back to the car park at Dent.

Barth Bridge, near Dent.

Walk 2
KIRKBY STEPHEN

This very gentle undulating stroll leads through heavenly countryside as befits the name of the Eden Valley. It leads under and over majestic bridges, follows footpaths along river banks and along the route of a railway line closed for more than 40 years. Add to this the chance to visit a magnificent old church and marvel at the views across lush countryside with the haunting ruins of a 14th century Pele tower and you have a perfect walk. The final link in this jigsaw of perfection is to find places to picnic and to enjoy the sights, scents and sounds of an ever-varying fauna and flora. If this does not inspire a family walker then nothing will. Kirkby Stephen is described as the walking capital of the area and it certainly caters well for hikers who like to hurry and strollers who like to saunter.

The Ratten and Rush, situated close to the Tourist Information Centre, is open from 10 am to 5 pm. The food is excellent, and the bacon, eggs and especially the Cumberland sausage will provide enough energy to keep you going all day, and there is always a vegetarian soup. Tea and cakes are also served. Telephone: 017683 72123.

DISTANCE: 4 miles
TIME: Allow 2½ hours
MAP: OS Explorer OL19
STARTING POINT: The Market Square in Kirkby Stephen (GR 775088).
HOW TO GET THERE: Kirkby Stephen is reached via the M6 turning off at Junction 40. Follow the A66(T) for about 15 miles to Brough and then turn onto the A685 signed Kirkby Stephen. This is reached in around 8 miles. There is plenty of parking in the town. There is free parking on the Market Square close to the church except on Mondays, which is the busy market day and has been since the 14th century.

THE WALK

 1. Start at the cloisters in the Market Square.

These cloisters were built in 1810 and financed by a local lad made good. John Waller was a naval purser and his intention was to provide a shelter for churchgoers and market traders and it soon became famous as a butter market. Take time to pass through the cloisters to the church of St Stephen. This has Saxon origins but the present structure is mainly Norman. It is of huge proportions and is rightly known as the Cathedral of the Dales. To the right of the church path is the Trupp stone, a flat slab on which, up until 1836, tithes were paid. Inside the church is the famous Loki stone, which is carved with Anglo-Danish symbols, the only such structure in Britain and one of only two remaining in Europe.

From the cloisters, turn left. Pass the public toilets and a small free car park on the right.

2. Descend the narrow winding road and follow the obvious signs down a flight of steps to Frank's Bridge. This is said to be named after Francis Birkbeck who was a wealthy brewer operating in the early years of the 19th century. To the right of this footbridge is a charming cottage renovated in 2005. Cross the bridge and turn right along a very pleasant riverside footpath with the Eden on the right and lots of seats on the left. Follow this footpath and pass through woodland.

3. Turn right and descend to the river. Cross by means of an elevated footbridge and turn left. The river is now on the left. Follow a track through mature woodland. The path then sweeps uphill and to the right and approaches Stenkrith Bridge.

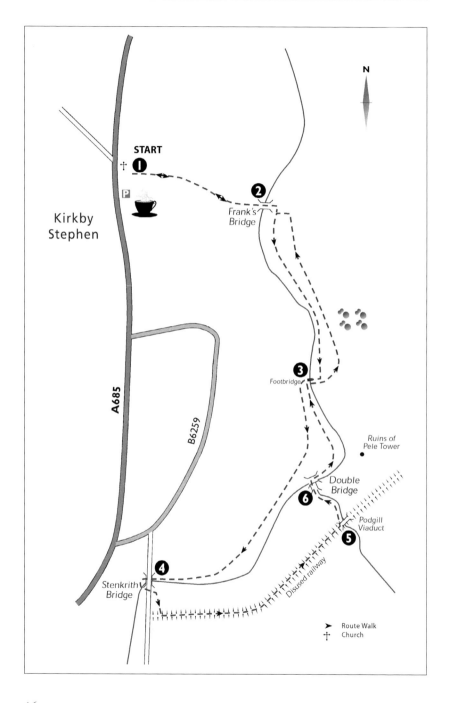

Frank's Bridge, Kirkby Stephen.

4. Cross the bridge and turn sharp left. For the next 1½ miles the route follows the dismantled track of the old railway. This railway began life in 1857 and was once the main line linking Darlington with the iron ore mines of north Lancashire. The line closed in 1962, but Kirkby Stephen still has a station on the Settle to Carlisle line which is situated about 1 mile to the south and above the town centre.

5. Leave the old railway track by turning left at the famous Podgill viaduct. The viaduct has very recently been restored by a hard working trust and it is worth a diversion of just a few yards to view it. Follow the clearly-marked footpath.

6. Pass under a double bridge and ascend an embankment. Look to the right to see the site of a Pele tower at Hartley built in the 14th century as a defence against the invading Scots. The path veers to the right and then turns right over the footbridge crossed at point 3. Turn left and return to Frank's Bridge and on to the starting point.

17

Walk 3
LITTLE SALKELD

This is a lively undulating stroll, which not only has stunning scenery, haunting history and wonderful wildlife, but also provides inspiring sound. There is nothing to beat the sound of a watermill in full flow unless it is the sound of bird song. Little Salkeld is one of those rare villages, which is truly caught in its own time warp and does not even have a pub. This does not matter because the stroll begins and ends at a unique teashop!

The Watermill Organic Tearoom & Millshop is an integral part of the working watermill. Its menu is vegetarian and all the food on offer is of local origin. The flour to make the bread and cakes has been ground in the mill and bags of home-milled flour can be purchased from the shop.

The soups are excellent, especially the potato and watercress variety, and all are served with a choice of six different types of bread, one of which has a cheese and onion flavour. The tea and coffee are excellent and it is a great feeling to eat lunch with the sound of grain being ground and the smell of bread being baked! Telephone: 01768 881523.

Long Meg and her daughters.

DISTANCE: 3 miles
TIME: Allow 2 hours
MAP: OS Explorer OL 5
STARTING POINT: The car park at the watermill (GR 568360).
HOW TO GET THERE: From the M6 leave at junction 40. Follow the A686 for
about 4 miles. Turn onto the B6412 to Langwathby and continue on this road
through the village. Little Salkeld is reached in about 1½ miles. Cross a bridge
with the road bearing left. The watermill and car park are less than 200 yards on
the right. The watermill building is known locally as the Pink Mill and is open
daily except Christmas day and Boxing day.

THE WALK

☕ **1.** From the car park explore the mill and perhaps enjoy a guided
tour of the machinery, and a meal. Be sure to ask if you wish to walk from
the mill. If you do not want to eat here, or visit the mill, there is some street
parking in the village.

*The word Salkeld means 'the spring by the willow trees' and this is still an
accurate description. The mill began to thrive when the defeat of Bonnie
Prince Charlie in 1745 brought peace to the border country and*

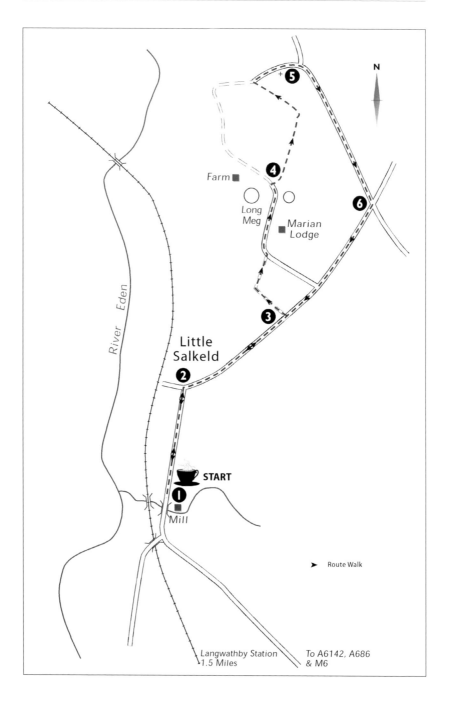

N

Farm ■

Long
Meg

○

■ Marian
Lodge

6

River Eden

Little
Salkeld

2

3

☕ START

1
■
Mill

➤ Route Walk

Langwathby Station
1.5 Miles

To A6142, A686
& M6

The bridge and mill at Little Salkeld.

businesses could function without worry. When the Settle-Carlisle railway opened in 1870 the mill continued to prosper but it declined from the 1930s as milling became dominated by a few large companies. Since 1975 the mill has been privately operated. The number of customers is now growing again, and the mill is doing well, with its flour being distributed throughout England.

From the mill turn right and ascend the narrow and steep village street.

2. At a T-junction turn right at a sign indicating Long Meg – Druids' Circle. Actually the term druid is not accurate as the circle is much earlier than the Celtic period but the name is haunting enough to be still used. Climb the steep minor road until a narrow track leads off to the left.

3. Although this track is not signed it is the first one to be reached and is less than ½ mile from the village. Turn left and continue a gentle climb. The footpath bears right after 300 yards. Continue for about the same distance to join a very narrow road. Pass Marian Lodge to the right and then over a cattle grid.

4. The circle of stones is approached, with the main group including Long Meg herself on the left and the minor group on the opposite side of the road.

The circle is privately owned, but visitors are free to visit. Remember, however, that this area is grazed by cattle. Long Meg herself is a tall sandstone structure. It has been suggested that Meg indicates a magus or magician. If so, it puts a whole new meaning to the term 'magic circle'. It could also, however, mean a megalith, and this one is surrounded by about 70 stones. It is considered bad luck to physically count the stones which are thought to be more than 3,500 years old.

From the farm track splitting the circle, a footpath bears right and then veers slightly left. Pass Maughanaby Farm on the left. Continue along the obvious path for around ½ mile.

5. Approach an ancient cross and a minor road which marks the site of St Michael's church, also called Addingham church. In medieval times some churches were sited away from the village. Some were sited in order to bury victims of the plague but in this case the original Addingham village kept being washed away by floods and higher, safer ground was chosen. All that remains here are gravestones and the old cross. Turn right and then right again along a minor road.

6. At a road junction, turn right towards Little Salkeld. Look to the right to see the site of Little Meg which is a much smaller circle and also on private land. The minor road descends into the village of Little Salkeld. Turn left and continue the descent back to the mill.

Walk 4
WETHERALL

This is a gentle meander through an unspoiled village. There is the chance to enjoy the sight of a unique church, follow in the footsteps of an 8th-century saint and also in those of the 12th-century Benedictine monks. Here are undulating footpaths through spectacular woodlands and be sure to savour the sound of a surging river. The birdlife is spectacular throughout the year with wintering wildfowl, spring migrants, summer songsters and autumn visitors. Kingfishers are resident close to the salmon traps built in the river by the monks in the 14th century. The balance here between history and natural history is irresistible.

Killoran Country Guest House and Tea Garden is situated opposite the village green. With extensive views over the River Eden from the rear, this is a wonderful place to enjoy a cuppa. The house was built in 1869 by John Scott and he added a tower to enable him to see Dixon's chimney which was then the tallest building in Carlisle. Until the late 1960s, the house was owned by Rolls Royce and it was here that guests from all over the world were entertained. Ballistic missiles were designed and discussed at meetings held here in secret.

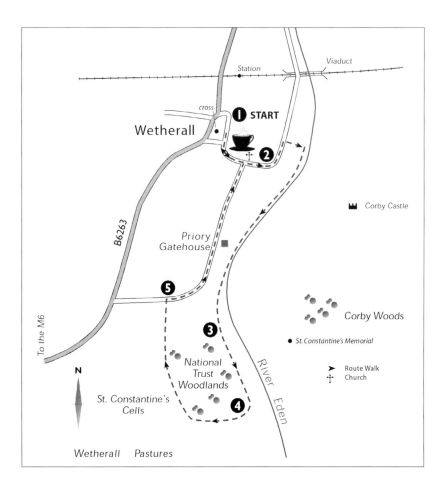

Thankfully, these days there is nothing secret about Killoran and it is an excellent place to enjoy an elegant brew of tea in spectacular and friendly surroundings. Telephone: 01228 560200.

DISTANCE: 3 miles
TIME: 2 hours
MAP: OS Explorer 315
STARTING POINT: The Tea Garden in Wetherall (GR 468545).
HOW TO GET THERE: Wetherall is situated close to the M6 and the best exit to use is number 42. Immediately off the motorway the first left turn indicates Wetherall along the B6263. After about 2½ miles Wetherall is reached, and there is parking alongside the substantial green dominated by an ancient cross.

The impressive five-arched railway viaduct, Wetherall.

THE WALK

1. Leave the teashop on the left and the old market cross on the village green to the right. Turn left and descend the steep narrow road to pass the church, also on the left.

The church, with the triple dedication to Holy Trinity, St Mary and St Constantine, is reached through a lych gate. St Constantine was a man who lived his hermit-like life in caves close by and he has only one church dedicated to him. The present church is a joy and its architecture is mainly 16th-century. Inside is a mausoleum of the Howards of Corby Castle. This was built in 1791 and there is a wonderfully carved memorial to Lady Maria Howard which inspired Wordsworth to write a sonnet to her memory.

2. Pass Ferry Hill House on the right with the five-arched railway viaduct straight ahead. Turn right and descend steeply through an area ideal for enjoying a picnic by the river.

As its name implies Ferry Hill House was the home of the ferryman. He rowed travellers over the Eden before bridges were built in the 18th century and before the railway came in 1830.

The gatehouse is all that remains of Wetherall Priory.

3. Follow the well-marked footpath keeping the river on the left. Pass into the well-maintained National Trust woodlands.

Look up to the left for views of Corby Castle with its 13th-century keep. A life-sized statue of St Constantine can be seen close to the river.

4. Turn sharp right and climb steep steps leading up from the river and then sharp right again. Look to the left for the Wetherall Pasture where the monks once grazed their livestock. It is here also that caves can be seen and which are still referred to as St Constantine's Cells. Continue uphill crossing a stile and passing through a gate.

5. At the junction of the B6263 turn right onto a quiet, minor road. This leads to the famous gatehouse which is all that remains of Wetherall Priory.

Some of the stones from the priory have no doubt been incorporated into the adjacent farm buildings. The Priory was a Benedictine house founded in 1106 as a daughter house of St Mary's Abbey in York. It was dissolved by Henry VIII between 1536 and 1539. The Gatehouse, however, was used as the vicarage for Wetherall church until around 1780 and is now preserved by English Heritage and is available to view at all times.

Continue along the narrow road and return to the centre of Wetherall.

Walk 5
BIRDOSWALD AND HADRIAN'S WALL

In 2004, the 84-mile length of Hadrian's Wall was opened as a long distance footpath. The new sections of the footpath had been opened thanks to the efforts of local councils and English Heritage.

It is now possible to enjoy a circular route from the fort at Birdoswald. This leads across lush green fields overlooking sweeping swathes of moorland and alongside mineral springs once popular with those in search of a miracle cure. The miracle cure these days can be found by walking the wall and soaking up the rich history and natural history.

The teashop at Birdoswald is part of the Roman fort museum-complex which consists of a shop selling books and maps and a neat little café. This was converted from a cow byre and hay barn dating from 1745. There is a spacious outdoor eating area which was once the farmyard. Soup and sandwiches are available, the locally baked 'slab cakes' make it worth a visit just to sample them even without the added bonus of a real slice of Roman history. Before setting off on the walk why not take with you a bottle of Hadrian's Spring Water which is sold here? The complex is open daily from April until October and on most weekends throughout the year. Telephone: 016977 47602.

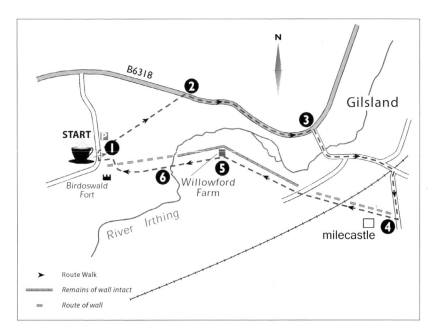

DISTANCE: 4 miles

TIME: Allow 3 hours

MAP: OS Explorer OL43

STARTING POINT: The Information Centre at Birdoswald (GR 615665).

HOW TO GET THERE: Birdoswald is signed directly off the A69 about halfway between Carlisle and Hexham. Prominent brown signs clearly indicate the turn which is less than ½ mile from the road. The OS map shows only one car park but there are now two including a coach park (Pay & Display). The Fort and Information Centre can be seen from the car park.

THE WALK

 1. Start from the Information Centre at Birdoswald.

The visitors centre (entry fee payable) is well worth a visit. Audio visual displays have been prepared by English Heritage and this is the place to help set Hadrian's Wall into context. The wall was not intended to be a battle zone but simply to mark the northern outpost of the Roman Empire. The instigator was the Emperor Hadrian (AD 76–AD 138).

Armed with a knowledge of history, descend from the Fort to the car park,

This milecastle at Poltross Burn is very well preserved.

from which an obvious footpath leads gently uphill. Keep looking behind to see the wall, and the ditch which followed its course.

2. The footpath meets the minor road (B6318). Turn right and follow this road for just over ½ mile towards Gilsland.

The wall can be seen below to the right. Uphill and to the left are a number of little streams, some of which smell of hydrogen sulphide. The Victorians thought that what smelled bad had to do you some good and for several years Gilsland was a very important spa.

3. At Gilsland turn right into the village but look up to the left to see the old buildings which were built to attract guests in search of a cure. Several have now been converted into hotels. In the village, continue along the B6318 and look to the right for an obvious footpath sign indicating Poltross Burn and Milecastle. A grassy track ascends steeply to the left and then bears right. Follow the very obvious sign to the right. This passes through a narrow ginnel and then ascends steeply to Poltross Burn which is dominated by a railway viaduct which crosses the valley.

4. Ascend a steep track which leads to the milecastle on the left.

This is one of the best preserved 'milecastles' along the wall so do take time to explore it and to read the explanatory boards provided by English Heritage.

Along the Roman wall at Willowford.

The only track continues to a kissing gate. Turn right through this and follow the instructions to cross the railway line. Pass through a second kissing gate and descend a lush field. Ahead is the old rectory and also the wall. Approach the wall and turn left onto a track created as part of the new footpath.

5. Follow the wall to Willowford Farm. Here the wall and the path descend steeply to Willowford Roman Bridge.

Look for a plaque on the farm wall indicating the Roman legion which built this stretch of the wall. This is written in English but above is the Roman original. These days the span is high and dry which indicates that the River Irthing has changed its course over the centuries and is now around 100 yards to the right. The explanatory drawing on an indicator board here shows that this bridge was one of the largest and most important in Britain.

6. Follow the track leading to a new iron footbridge over the Irthing. Cross this and continue along the wide meandering path which then sweeps right before ascending steeply to meet the line of the wall once more. Here the wall and the path turn sharp left and lead directly to Birdoswald Fort and the car park.

Walk 6
GOSFORTH

This gently undulating stroll provides splendid views of coast, woodland and sweeping fertile farmland. It passes old and distinguished farmhouses, an ancient church and a very fine Christian cross dating from the 10th century. The tiny village of Gosforth is liberally provided with pubs and hotels which all provide a welcome for walkers. The circuit is suitable for families and is dog-friendly whilst there are so many places to picnic that one is spoilt for choice. Naturalists will enjoy every step of the route, which passes through areas of woodland, lush fields and moorland.

 Ramblers of Gosforth Tearoom and Gift Shop, as its name implies, caters for ramblers and is open daily from 9.30 am to 5 pm except Mondays. On offer is freshly prepared home-made food using local produce. There are light lunches, jacket potatoes, all day breakfasts, scones and cream teas served in spacious surroundings. On hot days there is a small open-air spot and the locally made ice cream is excellent. Telephone: 019467 25258.

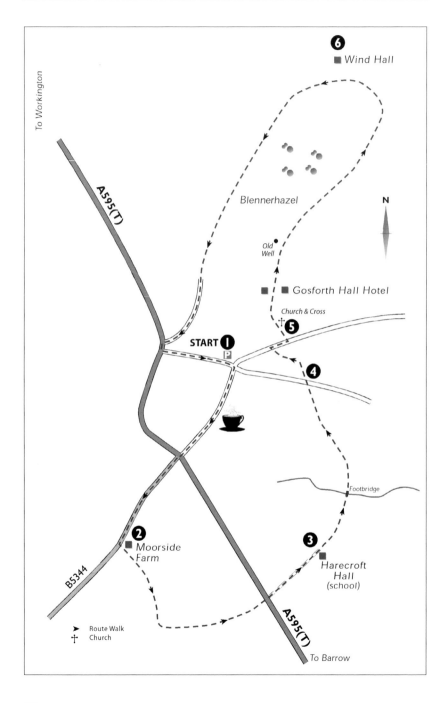

To Workington

A595(T)

6
■ Wind Hall

N

Blennerhazel

Old Well

■ ■ Gosforth Hall Hotel

Church & Cross
† **5**

START **1**
P

4

Footbridge

2
■ Moorside Farm

3
■ Harecroft Hall (school)

B5344

➤ Route Walk
† Church

A595(T)

To Barrow

St Mary's church at Gosforth.

DISTANCE: 3½ miles
TIME: Allow 2½ hours
MAP: OS Explorer OL3 and OL6
STARTING POINT: The car park in Gosforth (GR 068037).
HOW TO GET THERE: Gosforth is easily reached from the A595 which links Millom with Workington. Turn off along a minor road signed Gosforth. The village is less than a mile from the A595. At the crossroads bear left and then right. The car park is about 100 yards on the left. There is an information board and toilets.

The Walk

1. Turn right into the village, where there are three pubs which dominate its square. These are the Globe, the Lion and the Lamb, and the Wheatsheaf. These are all excellent places for snacks and drinks. Bear right and pass the Ramblers café on the left. Continue to reach the A595. Cross this and continue straight ahead along the B5344.

2. Just beyond Moorside Farm, on the left, is a stile leading across a field to a second stile.

Look behind to see the towers of Sellafield, which is the major employer in the area. Beyond this nuclear complex the Isle of Man can be seen on

33

most days of the year. Straight ahead is Black Combe and to the left are the majestic fells of Wasdale.

The path winds its way through fertile fields. This is one of several places on this walk to watch for breeding oystercatchers. Reach and cross over the A595 and look out to the left for the impressive Victorian buildings of Harecroft Hall School.

3. Pass through a gate and cross a well-marked footpath through a field. Cross a small footbridge over a stream. Look out for resident dippers and grey wagtails, and in the summer this is the haunt of common sandpipers. The footpath veers gently to the left.

4. At a minor road, cross and then veer left along a footpath with Gosforth village visible to the left. The footpath reaches another minor road. Turn right and follow the road for around 200 yards.

5. Look for St Mary's church on the right. Pass through the lych gate and in a few yards you will see the tall slender Gosforth cross.

This Viking cross is 14 ft high, made of red sandstone, and is set in its original 10th-century socket. Its carvings are a curious mixture of Christian and Norse symbolism as if the sculptor was not sure which religion to follow and decided to hedge his bets.

Inside the church are carved stones of a similar date as well as two hogback tombstones also typical of the Viking period. The church itself is an impressive mixture of Norman and Early English styles.

From the church turn right and pass through the complex of buildings making up Gosforth Hall Hotel. This dates to 1658 and the building itself and the stable block are in an excellent state of preservation. Pass through a gate and follow the signs indicating Wind Hall. Ascend through splendid woodland and to the left of the path is an ancient well which is said to date back to Saxon times.

6. Pass through an area called Blennerhazel and, as Wind Hall is approached, the path sweeps left. Blennerhazel is now on the left. Pass through a series of stiles and gates along an obvious footpath and descend through a belt of trees back to the village. Turn left to reach the car park.

The Viking cross at Gosforth is 14 ft high.

Walk 7
MARYPORT

This route follows spectacular coastal scenery from sea level to the soaring cliff top. Seabirds and flowers are everywhere in the warmer months whilst a winter walk also has its typical fauna and flora. All around is history which would have been familiar to Wordsworth whose publisher was a resident of Maryport. Here are the Georgian dwellings of rich merchants and ship owners interspersed with hotels frequented by Dickens. Streets of old cottages lead up from the harbour to the cliffs. These cliffs provided watchtowers for the Celts during the Iron Age and the Romans had a large fort on a headland and a port on the estuary of the River Ellen. Don't miss the glories of a stroll round Maryport and make sure not to be rushed.

☕ The spacious café at the Lake District Coast Aquarium overlooks the recently renovated harbour area. It is open all the year round from 10 am to 5 pm. It offers a varied menu and local produce usually features among the choices on offer. There is a fee to enter the aquarium itself but there is much to see, with lots of exhibits dealing with the local environment and is well worth a visit. Telephone: 01900 817760.

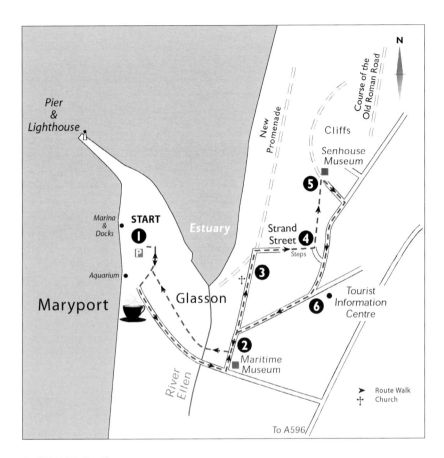

DISTANCE: 3 miles

TIME: Allow 2 hours for the walk and extra time to explore the aquarium and museums.

MAP: OS Explorer OL4

STARTING POINT: The Lake District Coast Aquarium, Maryport. (GR 034366).

HOW TO GET THERE: From the Cumbrian coast follow the A596(T) signed to Maryport. Descend into the town with obvious signs leading down to the harbour. Cross the bridge over the River Ellen. Sweep right into a very large Pay & Display car park opposite the aquarium.

THE WALK

1. From the aquarium and its teashop turn right and head towards the town.

The old harbour at Maryport is worth taking the time to explore.

First, though, take time to explore the old harbour which, in the last few years, has had a major facelift. In the early 1750s there were only a few fishermen's cottages along the estuary of the River Ellen but local landowner Humphrey Senhouse realised the potential of Ellenfoot for development and named his new town Maryport after his wife. By the early 1800s the new docks were thriving and iron works, glass works, paper mills, breweries, tanneries and shipyards were all doing a roaring trade.

2. Cross the bridge over the Ellen with a new and very attractive sculpture overlooking the river and the Maritime Museum.

This museum building was once a sailors' alehouse called the Queens Head. This is the place to discover the history of the port, which was the home town of Thomas Henry Ismay, the founder of the White Star shipping line, which operated many of the most famous transatlantic liners.

From the museum turn left to reach the Victorian church outside of which are a couple of old cannons and an anchor surrounded by flowerbeds.

3. From the church a new promenade has been built which is now part of the Cumbrian Coastal Path, a perfect haunt for serious botanists. Our route follows the well-named Strand Street which once marked the tidal limit before the recently constructed promenade was built. The Senhouse Roman Museum is clearly signed from here.

4. Turn right at a footpath sign to the Roman Museum and climb a long flight of steep steps. At the top of the steps turn left with the museum still clearly signed. Look left from the cliff top down to the harbour and in around ¼ mile approach an impressive building and a car park.

This is the Senhouse Roman Museum. It is open every day from 10 am to 5 pm at weekends and between July and October but other times vary, so it is best to telephone (01900 816168). An entry fee is payable and there is a shop which sells books, gifts and very light refreshments. The Senhouse family began collecting Roman artefacts from the old Roman fort as early as 1570. Since 1990, the museum has been run by a trust. What is unique about this museum is that it holds the best collection of altars dedicated to Roman gods to be found anywhere in the world.

5. From the museum retrace the route for less than 300 yards. Turn left and then right along very minor roads lined with terraced houses. Descend very steeply to a road junction into the heart of the town.

6. With the new Tourist Information Centre on the left, turn right and return to the Maritime Museum (now on the left). Cross the bridge over the River Ellen and turn right back to the Aquarium and the car park.

The Maritime Museum at Maryport.

Walk 8
COCKERMOUTH

This route follows the meanders of the River Cocker just before its confluence with the Derwent in the centre of the town. It crosses lush fields, over and under majestic bridges, passes idyllic picnic spots and along a stretch of old railway track now fast becoming an important nature ramble. This is wonderful angling country much loved by Bing Crosby who may well have thought of Cockermouth as he sang 'Gone Fishin'. It was, however, Frank Sinatra's daughter, Nancy, who sang about 'boots made for walking' and Cockermouth is certainly a delightful place to walk.

Norham House Teashop is situated opposite Wordsworth's House and is reached through a narrow alley. Norham House has a fascinating history. It was built in the early 18th century by John Christian. His grandson was Fletcher Christian who will be forever remembered as the leader of the mutineers on HMS *Bounty*. Fletcher was born in 1764 and used to play in what is now the tea garden. He is also remembered in the name of a nearby pub and ended his days around the Pitcairn Islands.

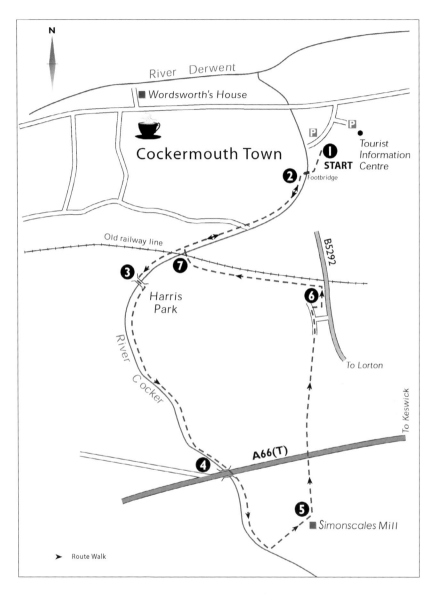

The tearooms are open daily from 9 am to 4 pm except on Sundays. The all-day breakfasts and fish and chips are famous and the children's menu is both sensible and appealing. The Cumbrian cream teas and sweets are also excellent but the real bonus is the setting and the atmosphere of these tearooms. Telephone: 01900 842330.

The River Cocker at Cockermouth.

DISTANCE: 3 miles
TIME: Allow 2 hours
MAP: OS Explorer OL4
STARTING POINT: The Riverside car park in Cockermouth (GR 126306).
HOW TO GET THERE: From the A66(T), follow the signs to Cockermouth. At a large roundabout look for the Lakeland Sheep and Wool Centre. Follow the town centre signs and descend into Cockermouth. At a T-junction with Wordsworth's House in front, turn right. Follow the main road to Market Place and turn right into Market Street. Follow the large car park signs close to the Tourist Information Centre. On the left is the Bitterbeck car park and to the right is the larger Riverside car park from where the walk starts. Both car parks are Pay & Display.

THE WALK

1. The impressive Tourist Information Centre and the town hall are reached from the car park by means of a set of steps. Here, too, is an excellent bookshop. Starting with your back to the Tourist Information Centre, and keeping the pretty little River Cocker to the right, look for a footbridge after about 50 yards.

2. Turn right over the bridge and then immediately left. A sign indicates Harris Park. The river is now on the left. A short distance to the right, and signed from the route, is the house where William Wordsworth was born. It is now run by the National Trust. Nearby is the teashop. The route follows the signs for Harris Park. After about 300 yards pass under a bridge and still keep the river on the left. Stroll through Harris Park.

3. At the end of the park pass through a gate and turn left onto a footbridge over the Cocker. Cross this and swing right following a pretty meander of the river now to the right and with lush fields to the left. This is an ideal habitat for naturalists to explore, with summering sandpipers, sand martins, swallows and swifts.

Follow this footpath for about ¾ mile.

4. Pass under a bridge which carries the A66(T) and follow the riverside path to Simonscales Mill.

5. At the mill turn very sharply left, leaving the river, and head under the A66(T) for the second time. Then follow a surfaced track passing a pleasant housing estate to meet the road linking Cockermouth with Lorton.

6. Cross this road and turn left. In less than 100 yards turn right to join an old railway track.

The Cockermouth, Keswick and Penrith Railway was built as a 31-mile track to carry coal, ore and metals between the industrial areas of Durham and west Cumberland. By 1865 tourist passengers were being carried but sadly the line closed in 1972. Since this time the area has developed into a linear nature walk.

Turn left and pass beneath a road bridge. Follow the track to the old railway bridge which spans the River Cocker. The views from here are spectacular.

7. Across the bridge turn right and descend a flight of steps. Turn right again and follow the obvious route back to the car park via the footbridge over the River Cocker mentioned in step 2.

Walk 9
BASSENTHWAITE

*W*oodland walks, an ancient church, lakeside scenery, the sound of rippling streams and birdsong, and perhaps the sight of an osprey in the summer, ensure that this level walk has a never-ending charm. The stately home of Mirehouse, featured on this route, is a mecca for those interested in English literature, but it is the glorious scenery around Bassenthwaite which is inspirational to those who walk these paths today. The lake here at Bassenthwaite is privately owned, and an entry fee is therefore payable, but this superb walk is well worth the modest charge. The house itself can also be visited (for an extra charge) but, since Mirehouse is family-owned, the opening hours are restricted. Telephone: 017687 72287. Bassenthwaite is, in fact, the only lake in the district which can correctly be called a lake. All the other fresh water areas are called either 'water', 'mere' or 'tarn'. Bassenthwaite is therefore unique and every footstep taken around it is a joy.

The Old Sawmill Tearoom is housed in a mill that was built in 1880 to harvest the timber from Dodd Wood. Photographs of the working mill line the walls and fixed to the beams are the saws and other tools associated with the trade. Inside the accommodation is spacious whilst outside is an attractive eating area.

The food is excellent and has a real local flavour to it. The soup is always gluten free and suitable for vegetarians, and the main menu is varied. Cumberland sausage served with mustard is a specialty, whilst the local

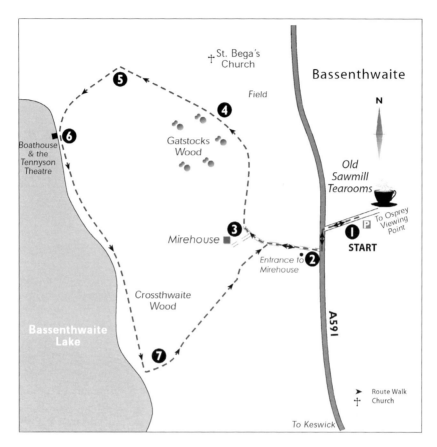

boiled ham is excellent. Puddings are exceptional so don't miss a slice of Aunty Grace's sticky gingerbread served with rum butter and ice cream.

The teashop, gardens and lakeside as part of this walk are open at weekends in the winter and daily from 19th March to 31st October. Tickets for Mirehouse can be obtained from the teashop which also sells books, maps and souvenirs. Telephone: 017687 74317.

DISTANCE: 2½ miles
TIME: 2 hours
MAP: OS Explorer OL4
STARTING POINT: The car park near the entrance to the Mirehouse estate (GR 236293).
HOW TO GET THERE: Mirehouse is 3½ miles north of Keswick on the A591 with
   Bassenthwaite Lake on the left.

The Tennyson Theatre on the banks of Bassenthwaite Lake.

THE WALK

☕ **1.** From the car park turn left for a few yards and then left alongside the A591. The entrance to Mirehouse is almost opposite.

From the car park woodland paths are marked to the right including the viewing point of the osprey nest site. This is looked after splendidly by the RSPB.

2. Cross the road and enter the Mirehouse estate (first ensuring that you have the entrance ticket which should be purchased at the teashop). Bear sharp right, cross a small stream and follow the marked signs indicating the house and the lakeside walk. Dogs are welcome on leads, whilst in the woodlands to the left are adventure playgrounds for children. This is the place to look out for red squirrel.

Mirehouse is reached on the left and a diversion of around 30 yards will reveal this splendid building. It is sometimes open to the public on payment of a small extra charge and it is still the family home of the Spedding family. The site has been occupied at least since Saxon times but the present house dates to 1666. Above the house stands Ullock Pike and Dodd Fell, long the haunt of buzzards soaring high above lifted by warm air currents. The Speddings played hosts to many famous literary figures including the Wordsworths, Thomas Carlyle and Tennyson.

3. Stay on the main footpath unless visiting the house and keep a stream on the right.

4. The path leads left through the woodland and the wide and obvious track heads towards Gatstocks Wood. From the open meadows to the right can be seen St Bega's church.

This fascinating building which can still only be reached by footpaths is dedicated to St. Bega an Irish princess and missionary washed up on the coast of Cumberland in the 9th century. She also gives her name to the coastal resort of St Bees. The present church has Saxon origins but is mainly early Norman and is seen at its remote best from this walk. Pass through Gatstocks Wood which is sure to delight naturalists.

5. The path now swings sharp left and soon the lakeside is reached. With the lake on the right, approach the boathouse and Tennyson Theatre.

This simple open-air theatre was established in 1974 with a reading of Morte D'Arthur. *It is known that Tennyson wrote the poem whilst staying with the Speddings at Mirehouse.*

6. Follow the idyllic and well-marked track first through woodland and then into an open area alongside the lake. Crossthwaite Wood is on the left. This is a breeding area for the jay, treecreeper, pied flycatcher and buzzard.

7. Approach a signpost indicating Mirehouse. Turn sharp left. Ascend a rocky but obvious footpath with fields to the right and left. This leads to splendid views of Mirehouse on the left. Pass through a metal gate and bear right. After about 200 yards a wider track is reached. Turn right and return to the entrance to Mirehouse. Cross the A591 and return to the teashop and car park.

Walk 10
KESWICK

This walk leads through long established woodlands and onto elevated viewpoints overlooking Derwentwater and Keswick. There are vistas of Skiddaw, Blencathra and Catbells high above. The route follows the banks of Derwentwater to Friar's Crag, so beloved of John Ruskin and Canon Rawnsley, the co-founder of the National Trust. Add to this the wonderful fauna and flora of the area and the popular theatre on the lakeside and you truly have a walk to suit all tastes.

The Lakeside Tea Gardens has a large interior but the colourful outside area is the real joy. There are open views to the landing stage from which cabin cruisers offer trips around Derwentwater and rowing boats may be hired.

The food on offer varies and the choice of hot meals includes those with a Cumbrian 'flavour'. Baked jacket potatoes come with a wide variety of fillings, and sandwiches can be made to order, which is ideal for walkers planning a picnic. Dogs on leads are made welcome, with bowls of water provided for them. The tea gardens are open every day from 10 am to 5 pm. Telephone: 017687 72293.

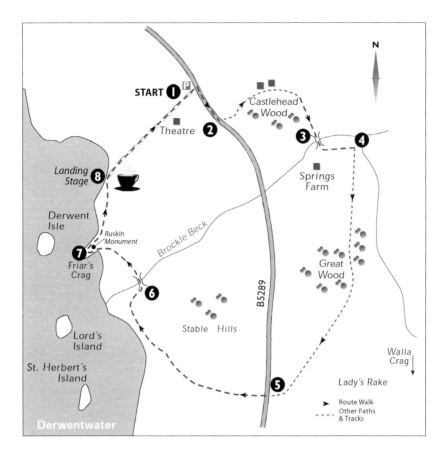

DISTANCE: 4 miles

TIME: 2½ hours

MAP: OS Explorer OL4

STARTING POINT: The large Pay & Display car park in the centre of Keswick (GR 266229).

HOW TO GET THERE: Approach Keswick via the A66(T) and turn off to the town and the A591. From the centre of Keswick the large Lakeside Pay & Display car park is signed from the B5289.

THE WALK

1. From the car park head out away from the lake to meet the B5289. Cross the road and turn right. In around 250 yards a sign to the left indicates the National Trust owned Castlehead Wood.

49

The pier on Derwentwater at Keswick.

2. Enter the woods and ascend a steep path leading to the top of Castlehead.

Take time to enjoy the views from this point. There is a marker sign to help identify them. The sharp profile of Catbells is seen at its best from here, as is Derwentwater, which laps at the foothills.

Pass houses on the left.

3. Cross a footbridge over Brockle Beck with Springs Farm on the right. Ascend through an area of mixed woodland. In gaps through the wood can be glimpsed panoramic views of Derwentwater.

4. The route turns right and crosses over a stile into the well-named Great Wood. This stile is tall and substantial with a hinged dog flap (allowing them to pass through without having to climb). Look up to enjoy views of Walla Crag or gaze down to appreciate the flowers in spring and summer, the colourful autumn fungi or, in winter, liverworts and mosses. Descend steeply through this well-signed area.

5. Turn sharp right and cross the B5289. The footpath bears right with the mixed woodlands of Stable Hills to the right and the shoreline of Derwentwater to the left.

Derwentwater ranks third in size of the Cumbrian lakes and is 3 miles long, 1½ miles wide and has a maximum depth of 75 feet but its average depth is only around 20 feet. Look out to the left to reveal the three islands spread like a string of pearls along the route. Derwent Isle was once the base of German miners who worked the area from the 17th century whilst St Herbert's Island was named from a pre-Norman saint who lived there as a hermit.

Follow the obvious footpath along the lakeside for just over ½ mile – there are lots of beautiful places along here to enjoy a picnic.

6. Pass along a footpath through a wooden gate and over a footbridge across a stream. Here the path diverges. Take the left fork and ascend a set of steps to reach Friars Crag. This is dominated by a memorial obelisk to John Ruskin (1819–1900).

☕ **7.** Around the monument bear right and continue along an obvious path through majestic trees, with views through to Derwentwater. On the right look for a plaque commemorating the life and work of Canon Hardwick Drummond Rawnsley (1851–1920) the co-founder of the National Trust. The Trust still oversees the well-being of this wonderful area. The path opens out to reveal the landing stage with launches and rowing boats. To the right of the landing stage is the Lakeside Tea Gardens. Best not to rush either the brew or the view from the gardens.

8. Ascend the metalled track turning right and passing the Lake Theatre on the right. Return to the car park.

Walk 11
POOLEY BRIDGE

This contrasting stroll follows a bank of one of the Lake District's unsung rivers which is rich in wildlife and passes through pasture and woodland. It climbs to the summit of the evocatively-named Dunmallard Hill, one of the most impressive Iron Age forts in the north of England. The steep descent winds its way through trees, but with plenty of open aspects to reveal the splendours of the Helvellyn range of mountains and panoramic views of Ullswater.

Granny Dowbekins Tearooms are set around a splendid garden overlooking Pooley Bridge and the River Eamont. Away to the left is Ullswater. Walkers are welcome and there is an excellent take-away service for those who want a picnic with a difference. There are no plastic cups here and the cream teas are mouth-watering. Breakfasts are also beautifully presented, as are the jacket potatoes with a variety of fillings. Telephone: 017684 86453.

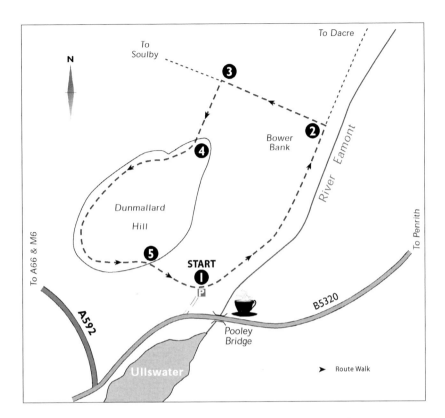

DISTANCE: 2½ miles

TIME: Allow 2 hours

MAP: OS Explorer OL5

STARTING POINT: The large Pay & Display car park by the river at Pooley Bridge (GR 468245).

HOW TO GET THERE: From the M6 motorway leave at junction 40 onto the A66. Just beyond the Rheged Discovery Centre on the left, turn sharp left onto the A592 signed Ullswater. After about 3 miles turn left along the B5320 signed Pooley Bridge. Just before reaching the bridge over the Eamont a prominent sign leads directly into the car park.

THE WALK

The car park is the starting point for a number of walks along well-marked routes some of which are along permissive tracks and not marked on all maps. The area is a real mecca for historians and

Pooley Bridge.

naturalists. Here is a splendid old bridge dating to 1763, when it cost £400 – a substantial sum in those days. Pooley actually means 'a pool by the hill' which is a very accurate description. The Eamont hereabouts is deep and wide and full of fish, which attracts wildfowl such as goosander and goldeneye, especially in winter. The river and Dunmallard Hill, which overlooks it, provides the birds with shelter when the winds drive snow across Ullswater. There are many walker-friendly cafés and pubs in the village just across the bridge.

1. From the car park take the signed footpath to Dacre and follow this wide and wooded track with the Eamont to the right.

2. After around ½ mile, look for a track leading off to the left. This is within the area known as Bower Bank.

3. Head towards the hamlet of Soulby but in less than ½ mile turn left along a field and ascend a well-marked track towards Dunmallard Hill.

4. This gentle climb leads up to Dunmallard Hill around which there is a circular and permissive path maintained by the National Trust. Turn right and enjoy splendid views of Ullswater and Helvellyn, with Pooley Bridge nestling below.

Dunmallard Hill is now covered in a mass of splendid old trees but in the Iron Age there was a hill fort at the summit. Traces still remain of what must have been a magnificent look-out area some 3,000 years ago, long before the Romans came a-calling to disturb the lives of the Celts.

Keep following the obvious path through the woods as it curves gently to the left.

This is the place to look out for red squirrels, great spotted woodpeckers and treecreepers, all of which are resident here.

5. Approach a signed and obvious path. Turn right and descend steeply back to the car park.

Walk 12
AIRA FORCE

This undulating walk affords the sight of a gentle lake away in the distance, expanses of mixed woodland, plus two of the most impressive waterfalls to be found in the region. The area is managed by the National Trust and the steep paths are maintained in good order (as are the useful handrails) which ensures safety for all, including families and dogs. The latter, however, should be kept on a lead. This walk is not only visually impressive but the sound of crashing white water is perhaps even more inspiring.

The Wells Teashop is a neat and well-appointed café. It is situated close to the car park at Aira Force and has an excellent garden whilst the interior is spacious. There is a shop selling local maps and books, plus sweets, especially the mouth-watering fudge.

The tearooms are open daily from 10 am to 5 pm between Easter and mid-October. It is jointly run by the Royal Hotel at Dockray and the telephone number is the same for both establishments. There is some

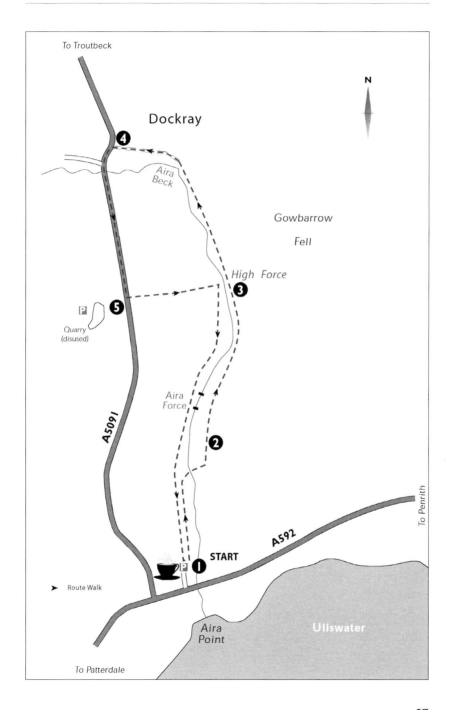

To Troutbeck

N

Dockray

4

Aira Beck

Gowbarrow

Fell

High Force

3

P

5

Quarry
(disused)

A5091

Aira Force

2

To Penrith

START

P **1**

A592

➤ Route Walk

Aira Point

Ullswater

To Patterdale

winter opening so it is worth ringing prior to a visit since, of course, the Royal Hotel is open all year round. The food on offer is of good quality and the home made soups served with hunks of bread are highly recommended. Telephone: 01768 482356.

DISTANCE: 3 miles
TIME: Allow 2 hours
MAP: OS Explorer OL5
STARTING POINT: Aira Force National Trust car park (Pay & Display) (GR 401201).
HOW TO GET THERE: From Penrith which is signed off the M6 (junction 41) turn left onto the A66 towards Keswick and Ullswater. With the Rheged Discovery Centre on the left continue for a short distance and then turn left along the Ullswater road (A592). Continue on this road ignoring the left turn to Pooley Bridge and follow the A592 with Ullswater on the left. Look out for the Aira Force Pay & Display car park sign on the right just before Glenridding.

THE WALK

☕ **1.** From the car park, stroll towards the substantial information point. Pass through a metal gate and follow the track with fields to the left and then veer right into an area of mixed woodland. Cross a footbridge over Aira Beck and turn left.

2. The track here is steep, but there are steps and handrails. Keep to the lower track and Aira Force is soon heard in the distance. Approach the first of two stone-arched bridges. Between the two bridges Aira Force tumbles around 70 ft creating a torrent of white water. Wordsworth and his sister Dorothy loved this spot and to them it was known as 'Airy Force'. The word 'force' is Scandinavian and simply means a waterfall.

Climb from the first to the second bridge by means of steps. Continue to climb past Aira Force, keeping the beck to the left.

3. The track leads to High Force on the left and Gowbarrow woods and fell to the right. Here, wild daffodils, much smaller than the cultivated variety, grow in profusion in the spring. It was here that Dorothy Wordsworth wrote wonderful prose in her diary about daffodils. Later her brother adapted his sister's words to produce the world famous poem *Daffodils* which still 'nod their heads in sprightly dance' in this historic area.

Pass the impressive High Force on the left and then continue through a delightful area of woodland. Pass through fields to reach a network of

Aira Force.

The higher bridge at Aira Force.

paths. Keep to the left as the track widens to reach the village of Dockray.

4. The route turns left just before the village.

It is, however, worth a short diversion of about a ¼ mile to enjoy this unspoiled Lakeland settlement. Dockray is dominated by the Royal Hotel which provides a warm welcome to visitors. Sailing on Ullswater and pony trekking can be arranged via the hotel.

From Dockray return to Aira Beck and follow the footpath to reach the A5091. Turn left.

5. After ½ mile, approach a car park situated in a disused quarry close to which is a footpath sign indicating Lower Pinetum. Here turn sharp left and cross fields leading down towards High Force. Turn right and keep Aira Beck on the left. Ahead and slightly to the right there are panoramic views of Ullswater. The stroll concludes via a steep descent to the car park. This steep descent, however, is aided by lots of steps and a few benches, well-sited to afford a second opportunity to enjoy the sound and sight of Aira Force.

Walk 13
GLENRIDDING AND HOWTOWN

This is a stroll with a difference because the circuit is completed by returning by boat from Howtown. The boat operates daily except Christmas Day and Boxing Day. It is a marvellously varied and undulating walk, passing through woodland and affording glorious views of the Helvellyn range towering above Glenridding. The trek is particularly wonderful in winter when the snow is on the hills whilst the chance to watch wildfowl along the section by the Ullswater shore is irresistible. All you need for this trip is your camera and binoculars and most importantly, the boat timetable! This can be obtained from Cumbria's Information Centres and many gift shops.

Ullswater Steamer Pier Teashop is a splendid place providing good food and stunning views of Ullswater at the Glenridding Pier and Information Centre. In addition there are small but comfortable bars and tearooms on each of the four pleasure craft which tour the lake throughout the year. Sitting and enjoying tea, coffee or something stronger, plus a bite to eat, while sailing the second largest lake in Cumbria, is a delightful experience. The same company operates the Fellbites café and restaurant in the village of Glenridding. Telephone: 017684 82229.

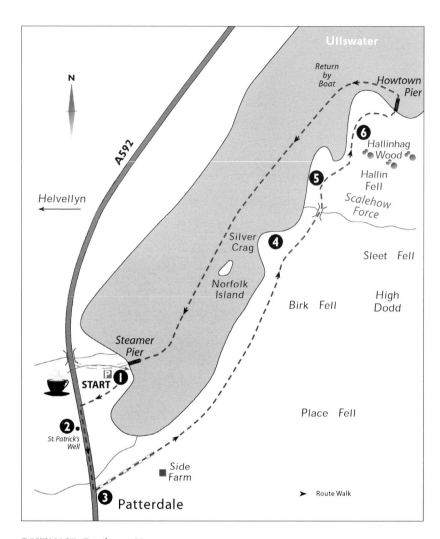

DISTANCE: 7 miles to Howtown

TIME: Allow 3½ hours but do remember to look at the boat timetable before you set off.

MAP: OS Explorer OL 5

STARTING POINT: The steamer pier car park at Glenridding (GR 387170).

HOW TO GET THERE: Approaching from Windermere in the south, follow the A592 over the Kirkstone Pass and down into Patterdale to the car park at the steamer pier at Glenridding. If travelling on the Keswick to Penrith road, turn off the A66 onto the A5091. This links to the A592 and the steamer pier car park.

View from the footpath at Glenridding.

THE WALK

☕ **1.** At the car park follow the large sign pointing left to Patterdale and Howtown. Pass through a gate and follow a well-marked path alongside and to the end of the lake where small boats can be hired. This path leads onto the A592. Turn sharp left along the pavement.

Ullswater is the second largest of the English lakes and is around 11 miles long and ¾ mile at its widest point. Its deepest point is 205 feet.

2. After about 300 yards, pass St Patrick's Well to the right. Another 300 yards brings you to a sign indicating St Patrick's church.

3. Ignore the route to the church, and look for a prominent sign pointing to Howtown. Turn left along this track and soon the busy village of Patterdale is left behind. Pass Side Farm on the right and bear left; the wide track is very obvious here. Look up to the right to see the impressive bulk of Place Fell which at 2,132 feet (656 metres) is a substantial mountain. As the path climbs, look left for splendid views of Glenridding and above it the Helvellyn range of mountains. Pass along an undulating path through mixed woodland towards Silver Crag.

MV Raven, one of the four pleasure craft that operate on the lake.

This is at about the halfway point of the walk and is the place to sit and enjoy the views of Ullswater and watch the boats passing Norfolk Island. It is also the place to look out for red squirrels.

4. Continue along the path and then down to Scalehow Beck. A short diversion upstream reveals a splendid little waterfall, Scalehow Force, concealed amongst the trees.

5. After visiting the falls, retrace your steps for around 200 yards and then cross a footbridge over Scalehow Beck. Follow the well-signed track through the tiny hamlet of Sandwick.

6. The path now passes through Hallinhag Wood and here is another chance to see red squirrels. Follow a gentle and well-signed path which descends to Howtown Wyke. Wyke simply means a bay and here is a convenient viewpoint from which the steamers can be seen approaching the pier. Meet the steamer here and return to Glenridding at leisure, making use of the steamer's 'mobile' teashop.

Walk 14
GRASMERE

This gentle circuit around Grasmere combines glorious scenery with towering hills and with gentle lakeside sections through trees and open clearings. Here too is a splendid old church alongside a crystal clear river and the last resting place of William Wordsworth and other members of his family. Strollers in search of a literary connection may be interested to seek out the memorial garden dedicated to the Wordsworths which was restored in 2005. And naturalists will love it in the winter when the shallow waters of Grasmere provide a rich feeding ground for the abundance of wildfowl and waders which flock here. Here then is a walk for all tastes and for all seasons.

The Rowan Tree has provided refreshment for visitors since Victorian times. The interior is spacious and the outside terrace overlooks the river Rothay and St Oswald's church. Here the service is excellent, and you will find lots of home baked produce. Sandwiches can be purchased either to eat here or take away, and the soup and roll is a substantial meal in itself. It is the atmosphere of the tea garden, however, which is worth travelling miles to enjoy. Telephone: 015394 35528.

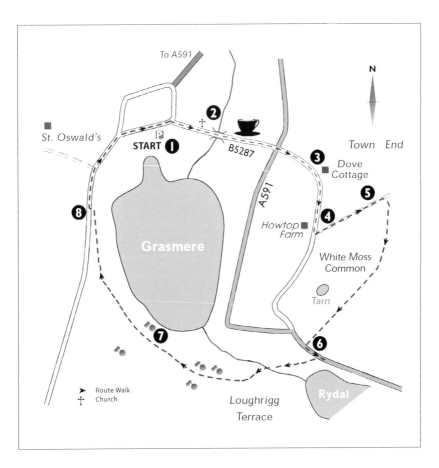

DISTANCE: 3½ miles
TIME: Allow 2½ hours
MAP: OS Explorer OL 7
STARTING POINT: The Pay & Display car park in Grasmere (GR 336073).
HOW TO GET THERE: Follow the A591 and turn off on to the B5287. Pass through the village ignoring the car park on the right. Cross over the bridge and see the church and river on the right. In a few yards turn left and after about 300 yards turn left to the Information Centre and Pay & Display car park.

THE WALK

1. From the car park and Information Centre turn right and then at the church turn right and explore St Oswalds.

The church of St Oswald in Grasmere is worth exploring.

Legend has it that the Saint preached on this spot as early as the 7th century. However, the present church dates from the mid-13th century with additions from the 16th century. This was the parish church of the Wordsworths, and William described the interior as a barn or even a forest. One can see what he meant. In 2005 the Wordsworth gravestones were made the focus of a memorial garden close to the river Rothay. On the opposite bank of the river is the tea garden of the Rowan Tree.

☕ **2.** Cross the bridge over the river and follow the minor road through the village to the A591. Cross the road and turn right.

3. In around 50 yards turn left and pass Dove Cottage on the left.

Developments during 2004 and 2005 have increased the area devoted to the Wordsworths and there is now a study area here in addition to an extensive library. Dove Cottage was once an inn called the Dove and Olive Branch alongside the old turnpike road connecting Ambleside and

Grasmere.

Keswick. The Wordsworths lived here from 1799 to 1808 and they landscaped the garden.

4. Follow the old turnpike road to Howtop Farm. Turn left up a tarmac road indicating Rydal. Continue to climb steeply but **do not** follow the sign for Alcock Tarn. Bear right and approach a row of cottages.

5. Turn right and descend the obvious but very steep footpath. Pass along White Moss Common and close to White Moss Tarn on the right. This is an area rich in natural history and buzzards are often to be seen soaring over the common on which there are a number of disused quarries. In the summer this is the breeding habitat of the wheatear.

6. At the A591, cross the road and turn left. In less than 100 yards turn right and descend to a footbridge. Cross the river Rothay and take the middle of three footpaths. This passes through an area of mixed woodland full of flora and fauna.

7. Ascend this path and in around ½ mile pass through a gate and turn right. Continue along an obvious path, which passes through another area of woodland to emerge onto the right hand bank of Grasmere.

This is the place to enjoy the birdlife, which is interesting at all times of the year, but especially so in winter. Grasmere is a shallow and very fertile lake and takes its name from Gris-mere, Gris meaning a pig. In Saxon times, wild boar frequented the woodlands. Grasmere is around one mile long, ½ mile wide and has a maximum depth of just 75 ft. This means that the water is full of nutrients and thus a haven for wildlife.

8. After ¾ mile along the lakeshore, turn through a kissing gate onto the minor Red Bank Road. Turn right and pass the St Oswald's Guest House complex on the left. Return to the car park and Information Centre.

The very pretty St Oswald's Guest House complex at the end of the walk.

Walk 15
CONISTON AND TARN HOWS

Coniston is a popular and historic village overlooked by Dow Crag and the Old Man. It is full of character and industrial archaeology. Peaceful footpaths lead out from the village into glorious countryside as this walk runs alongside bubbling streams, rippling waterfalls and mixed woodland towards and around Tarn Hows which is about a mile in circumference. Of all the walks in the Lake District this is one of real contrasts. It is a good idea to take a map with you so as to locate the mountains which enfold this area.

 The Coniston Dairy Tearoom is situated opposite the car park and information centre and is open daily from 9 am to 4.30 pm. It specialises in 'all-day breakfasts', and the soup of the day is a meal in itself. There is also some delicious ice cream, and the cream teas are a treat not to be missed. Local produce is used, and jam, honey and other farm produced goodies are available for sale. There are several types of tea and coffee on the menu and family groups are well catered for with a variety of sandwiches to take away for those who want to prepare their own picnic. Telephone: 015394 41176.

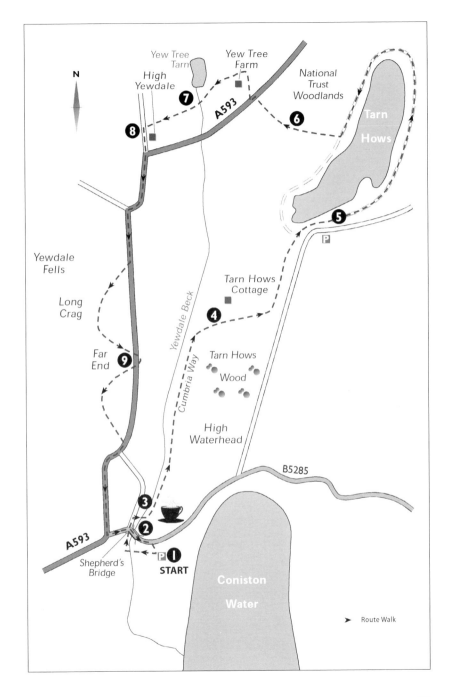

Yew Tree Tarn

High Yewdale

Yew Tree Farm

National Trust Woodlands

N

A593

Tarn Hows

7

8

6

5

P

Yewdale Fells

Tarn Hows Cottage

4

Long Crag

Yewdale Beck

Cumbria Way

Tarn Hows Wood

Far End

9

High Waterhead

B5285

3

2

A593

Shepherd's Bridge

P **1**

START

Coniston Water

➤ Route Walk

Tarn Hows.

DISTANCE: 6½ miles
TIME: Allow 3½ hours
MAP: OS Explorer OL 7
STARTING POINT: The Information Centre and Pay & Display car park in the centre of the village (GR 305974).
HOW TO GET THERE: Coniston is reached from Hawkshead on the B5284 and from Broughton-in-Furness and Torver along the A593. From Ulverston follow the A590(T) and turn off along the A5084 directly into Coniston.

THE WALK

1. From the car park follow the marked route towards Yewdale Bridge but, just before reaching this span, turn left. Pass the Primary school and cross Shepherd's Bridge.

2. At the end of the bridge steps lead up to and over a stile and then through a gate to an easy-to-follow footpath.

3. The route now follows part of the Cumbria Way. This is a 70-mile marked path linking Ulverston to Carlisle via Coniston, Langdale and Borrowdale. Follow the way markers with Yewdale Beck on the left and Tarn Hows Wood on the right. Take time during this climb to enjoy wonderful views of the mountains – the Langdales and Coniston Old Man. Follow the path as it clearly indicates right.

4. Keep to the right of Tarn Hows Cottage and then turn left parallel to a minor road to reach the Tarn Hows car park.

5. As you ascend a grassy footpath, the true majesty of Tarn Hows and the footpath which runs around it will be revealed to you.

It is hard to believe that this wonderful scene was created only in 1865 from three very small tarns. The idea was to 'enhance the landscape' and this certainly worked and is a delight to its human visitors and a perfect habitat for its water birds.

Follow the obvious footpath which winds round to the left. There are places here to sit and to enjoy a picnic. Above are views of the pointed peaks of the Langdales.

6. Pass through woodland until a footpath strikes off to the right. Look for waterfalls along a stream called Tom Gill. Pass through a kissing gate and cross a bridge to reach the road at Yew Tree Farm with its unusual circular chimney.

7. Cross a footbridge over the stream leading out of Yew Tree Tarn. Bear left and then turn sharp left to High Yewdale.

8. As you meet a narrow minor road, turn left and follow this road for about ¼ mile. Look for an obvious track on the right. This descends through an area of mixed woodland with Yewdale Fells high above to the right. It is the haunt of breeding great-spotted and green woodpeckers, and in summer the flowers and butterflies are a spectacle. Pass Long Crag on the right.

9. Approach an area well-named as Far End, and meet a minor road. Turn right onto another very short footpath before looping round to the right then left and right again to meet a crossroads. Turn right and the next right leads back to the starting point via Shepherd's Bridge.

Walk 16
WATERHEAD AND AMBLESIDE

This gentle walk is one of fascinating contrasts. At Waterhead, there are always lots of boats to watch. Pleasure steamers have been plying the 11 miles of Lake Windermere, from Lakeside to Waterhead, since 1845. Three substantial vessels, complete with cafés and bars, now operate the circular trip. They are the Tern (built in 1891), the Teal (1936) and the Swan (1938), and all have been carefully refitted and these days are powered by diesel. The Romans used the lake from AD 90 when they constructed a fort on the shore which they named Galava and which was home to 500 troops. Our stroll follows riverside paths to Rydal with its Wordsworth connections, and returns along winding footpaths back to the bustling village of Ambleside with its host of pubs, restaurants and teashops.

There can be very few teashops with a better view than the aptly named Pier Café as it looks out over the mooring stage and across the lake at Windermere. The café is open throughout the year, daily from 9.30 am to 5 pm, and offers everything from a well-brewed cuppa to substantial

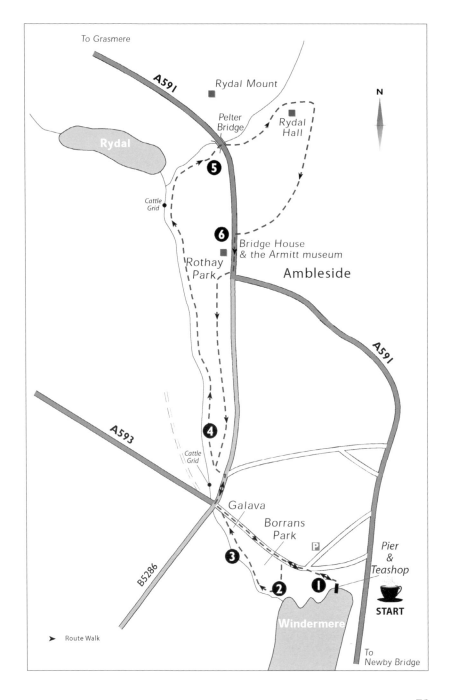

The pier at Waterhead.

meals, and it also has a licence to serve alcohol. My favourite repast is the Cumbrian tea, which consists of a sandwich, a scone with cream and jam plus a substantial pot of tea. There are plenty of mouth-watering, yet healthy, offerings for children, and the café also offers a take-away service for those who want to picnic.

DISTANCE: 5 miles
TIME: Allow 2½ hours
MAP: OS Explorer OL7
STARTING POINT: Waterhead Information Centre car park (GR 376033).
HOW TO GET THERE: From the M6 motorway, leave at junction 36. Follow the
 A590 and then the A591. Follow the A591 through Windermere towards
 Ambleside. Waterhead is to the left. For those wishing to combine their walk
 with a trip on the lake, there is a small car park to the left and close to the
 teashop and steamer pier. It closes at 6.15 pm. To the right is a much larger Pay
 & Display car park.

THE WALK

☕ **1.** From Waterhead pier turn left and follow the busy promenade with cafés and gift shops on the right and the lake with its jetties and rowing boats on the left. This is the place to watch people old and young fishing, and birds begging for food. Pass the Wateredge Hotel on the left and the Regent Hotel on the right.

2. Keep on the pavement to the left for about 50 yards beyond the Wateredge Hotel and look for a kissing gate in a wall to the left. Go through the gate and descend steps into Borrans Park.

Until 1834, Borrans was divided into three parts: Fisher Landing, Far Landing and Borrans Meadow. In 1925 the local council purchased all three and turned them into one public park.

Keep to the path on the left which then sweeps right. Take a moment here to gaze at the glorious views.

3. Look to the left of the path to find a short grassy track leading to a gate in a wall. Pass through the gate onto the National Trust owned site of Galava.

Only a few stones of the fort remain, and it is interesting to note that the Anglo-Saxon word 'borrans' means 'a pile of stones'. The views from the site are magnificent and there are Interpretation Boards here which will repay a few minutes' study.

From the Porta Principalis, bear slightly left and towards the River Rothay. Pass through another gate and then along an obvious boardwalk.

Continue on to reach the A593. Cross the road and bear left to the Rothay Manor Hotel and follow the signs indicating Keswick. Turn left at a car park and after about 70 yards pass behind the ambulance station. This leads to the river. Continue upstream through Rothay Park to Miller Bridge, keeping the river to your left.

4. At Miller Bridge join a track and turn right. After a cattle grid follow this road for about one mile keeping the river on the left. Cross another cattle grid close to Pelter Bridge where there is a small car park.

5. Cross the bridge at the A591. Turn left for a distance of only around 250 yards before turning right to Rydal Mount. This was one of Wordsworth's homes, and is worth visiting (fee payable). The route, however, follows a right turn to Rydal Hall. Part of this Grade II listed building dates to the 16th century and it is now the Diocesan Conference and Retreat Centre.

Windermere seen from Galava.

The panoramic parklands here are a treat, with the cascading waterfalls and the gardens laid out by Thomas Mawson around 1910.

Follow the footpath, of around one mile, through Rydal Park before reaching the A591.

6. Turn left and reach Ambleside in about 500 yards. Look out for the famous Bridge House near to which is the splendid Armitt Museum (small fee payable).

Turn right by the health centre down Stoney Lane to reach Miller Bridge. Then follow the river Rothay downstream towards Borrans Park and return to the starting point.

Walk 17
BROCKHOLE – WINDERMERE

This ancient and modern stroll begins at the Lake District National Park base at Brockhole. Leaving the A591 behind, it passes along very quiet bridleways, some of which were once important highways, possibly dating from the Bronze Age, and certainly improved and used by the Romans. Here are byways, barns and botanical treasures, wonderful woodlands, substantial houses and 18th-century cottages along with signs of a Celtic settlement. This gentle stroll offers all this plus the beautiful panoramic views over Windermere.

 The excellent teashop at Brockhole Visitors Centre is open daily from 10 am to 5 pm and offers meals to suit all tastes. Attached to the house is a garden terrace, which was built in the 1890s by William Henry Gaddum who made his fortune from the cotton industry. It is a joy to eat in, surrounded as it is by white painted walls which reflect the light onto the glorious display of colourful flowers in summer. The exterior of Manchester's cotton warehouses were also painted white. Before the days of electric lighting, customers could have their fabrics brought outside and would thus be better able to appreciate the colours. Next to the café is a well appointed information centre and shop selling gifts and maps.

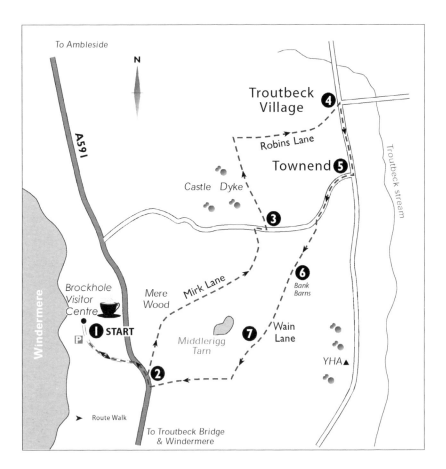

DISTANCE: 4 miles
TIME: Allow 2 hours
MAP: OS Explorer OL7
STARTING POINT: Brockhole Visitors Centre (GR 389008)
HOW TO GET THERE: From the A591 road, which links Windermere with
   Ambleside, a short drive leads to a Pay & Display car park.

THE WALK

☕ **1.** Firstly be sure to enjoy a stroll in the extensive grounds around
Brockhole, with well-signed access down to the pier from which pleasure
craft operate around Windermere Lake. The gardens have been designed
to provide interest and colour throughout the year. From the car park

The wonderful view over Windermere from Brockhole.

Townend is an interesting 17th-century home which is well worth visiting.

approach and cross the A591. At this point a bridlepath sign can clearly be seen.

2. Turn left along Mirk Lane. Pass Merewood Cottages and House on the left. This is a delightful stretch and passes the well-named Wood Farm. About ½ mile along a narrow path lined with trees, approach Holbeck Lane which is a quiet, narrow road. Follow this for a very short distance and then turn left.

3. This leads to the delightfully named track called Robin Lane.

Examine this very closely and you will see evidence of an ancient Celtic settlement, recognised by grassy mounds and which local people still refer to as the Castle. Robin Lane is of ancient origin connecting Troutbeck with Ambleside. It was part of a Roman highway which ran between the fort at Ambleside to the Penrith area and on to Hadrian's Wall.

Ascend gently to a National Trust sign indicating 'Martin's Wood'.

4. Robin Lane meets a minor road leading into the hamlet of Troutbeck. Turn right and head south along this road to a junction. Turn right and in just a few yards look for a National Trust car park and the entry to Townend (fee payable).

Time should be allowed to visit Townend, which is open from 1 pm to 4.30 pm Wednesday to Sunday (closed Monday and Tuesday) from Easter to the end of October. It was the home of a prosperous 17th-century yeoman but it is much more than this because there are even older barns and farm buildings. Inside are lots of oak panelling, contemporary furniture and a display of domestic implements of the period.

5. After visiting Townend, turn right along the narrow road for about ¼ mile.

6. At a bridleway sign, turn left along Wain Lane and descend towards Brockhole.

Enjoy the wonderful views of Windermere ahead whilst to the right and left are some magnificent old barns. Near the 18th-century house called Middlerigg is a man-made tarn excavated for farm stock in the early 1900s. This is the place for birdwatchers to keep a wary eye open for heron and wildfowl, and during the warmer months botanists travel miles in search of mosses, flowers and autumn fungi.

7. When Wain Lane reaches the A591, right turn and Brockhole is reached to the left in around 300 yards.

Walk 18
FELL FOOT AND GUMMER'S HOW

In 2004 the National Trust completed the restoration of Fell Foot Park, and created a circular walk along permitted footpaths. Today's walk follows the shores of Windermere before leaving Fell Foot and ascending to the 1,053 ft (321 metre) summit of Gummer's How. From this hill are magnificent views of Windermere spread out like a map with the Lakeside steamers and Fell Foot delighting the eye on a clear day. This is the place to hear cuckoos in the spring with the resident ravens and buzzards soaring above. Steam from the locomotives of the Lakeside and Haverthwaite railway can often be seen and also visible is the river Leven meandering its way out of Windermere. Add to this wonderful woodlands and crystal clear streams and you have perfection in sight and sound.

The Tearoom and National Trust shop are open daily from 11 am to 5 pm, and provide excellent fare. It was once a boathouse and looks out over the pier and an area from which rowing boats can be hired. Across the water can be seen the Lakeside steamer pier and a regular ferry service operates throughout the day between Fell Foot and Lakeside. Dogs are welcome here and drinking bowls are provided for them. Telephone: 015395 31273.

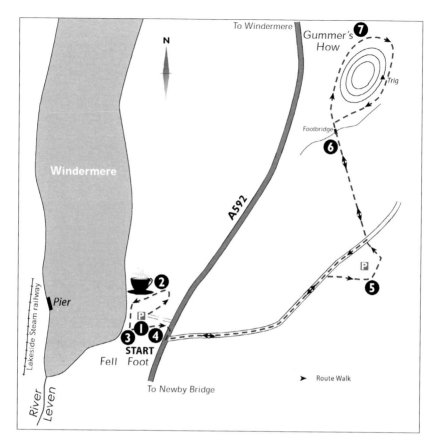

DISTANCE: 4 miles

TIME: Allow 3 hours

MAP: OS Explorer OL7

STARTING POINT: The Pay & Display car park (GR 386870)

HOW TO GET THERE: From the A590(T) turn right on the A592 just before Newby Bridge. In just over a mile look for a sign indicating Fell Foot Country Park to the left. Follow the signs to the park and, in about ½ mile, reach the Pay & Display car park.

THE WALK

1. These permissive paths were completed in 2004–5 and they are all well-signed. Bear right and then sweep gently down to the old boathouses and the teashop.

The steep climb up to Gummer's How.

☕ **2.** At the teashop turn left and pass the National Trust shop and the pier on the right. Bear left along the lakeside. There are well-placed seats here from which to enjoy the spectacular views to the steamer pier on the opposite side, and to watch the bird life which is fascinating in all seasons.

3. Turn left along a well-marked track leading towards the car park.

Display boards here make interesting reading as they explain some of the history of Fell Foot. It dates back at least to 1619 with the last house being demolished in 1907. On the display boards are photographs of the house in its heyday during the 1870s.

Continue to the car park and bear right.

4. At the A592 cross the road and turn right. In around 100 yards a minor road leads off left to Gummers How. This narrow, quiet road climbs steeply for around a mile but there are plenty of places to stop to admire views of mixed woodlands and panoramic views of the lake.

5. To the right of the road is Gummer's How car park. Go into the car park and follow a marked track up into woodland. This bears left and after 300 yards crosses the minor road. Pass through a wooden gate where a sign points to the summit of Gummer's How. This path climbs steeply.

6. Cross a footbridge over a stream and ascend a steep stony track. To the left are truly wonderful views of Windermere and Lakeside and in spring this is the haunt of cuckoo and ring ouzel. The path continues to climb but sweeps right to reach the summit of Gummer's How on the top of which is a trig point.

7. The path now swings right and descends to the footbridge. Turn left and descend to the minor road. Turn right, passing the Gummer's How car park on the left. Then return down the steep road and, on reaching the A592, turn right and then left to find the car park at Fell Foot.

The view from the top of Gummer's How is worth the climb.

Walk 19
CARTMEL

This stroll is a fascinating, and often awe-inspiring, mixture of history and natural history where a variety of plants and insects especially butterflies can be seen. It passes by a famous racecourse, through an unspoiled village, which is dominated by a medieval priory and dissected by a gentle little river, and then up and over an escarpment of limestone. The panoramic views are spectacular and include mountain, moorland and Morecambe Bay.

Market Cross Cottage was built in 1656 and, with its beamed ceilings, is very attractive. It is also a splendid teashop and the Lakeland special tea is well worth the trip, as are the toasted teacakes and crumpets. A good selection of coffees is also available. The impressive menu includes homemade Cumberland pie, local potted shrimps and scrambled egg with smoked salmon. The fish and chip choice usually involves local and very fresh plaice, and the homemade soup is substantial and most welcome on cooler days. Bed and breakfast is available. Telephone: 01539 536143.

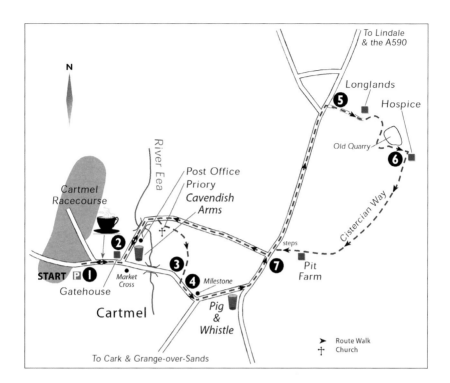

DISTANCE: 3½ miles

TIME: Allow 2 hours

MAP: OS Explorer OL 7

STARTING POINT: Cartmel racecourse car park. Apart from four days each year when racing is taking place there is plenty of parking at the racecourse. The small parking fee is payable by means of an honesty box (GR 376786).

HOW TO GET THERE: Cartmel is reached from Junction 36 off the M6 and then along the A591 and the A590. At the summit of Lindale Hill turn left to reach Cartmel along a very narrow road. Follow the signs through the village to reach the signed car park at the racecourse.

The Walk

1. Follow the narrow road into the heart of the village, pass the old market cross on the right and the teashop on the left.

2. After exploring the market square, turn left through the archway of the Priory gatehouse.

The racecourse at Cartmel.

The gatehouse was built by the monks around 1330 and was heavily fortified in an attempt to provide protection against the invading Scots. The gatehouse functioned as a porter's lodge, guardroom and, from one of its doors, alms were handed out to the needy. In the 18th century it was the local grammar school. The gatehouse is now looked after by the National Trust.

Continue along the narrow street and pass the 18th-century Cavendish Arms on the right and, as you reach the post office, glance across to take in the view of the solid magnificence of Cartmel Priory visible on the right. Cross Wheelhouse Bridge over the little river Eea and then follow a footpath to the right leading to the Priory.

This Augustinian priory was founded in 1190. The church contains some magnificent stained glass dating from the 15th century but the real treasure has to be the oak carvings. The misericords, in particular, are wonderfully carved. These hinged seats allowed the older brothers to rest during the services, which were often very long indeed. Cartmel was unusual in that its policy was to permit the local people to worship with the monks. Although the rest of the priory was destroyed during Henry VIII's dissolution of 1538, the church of St Mary and St Michael was saved. The Priory continues to function as Cartmel's parish church.

3. From the Priory leave by the metal gate onto the main street of the village. Turn left and continue along the road. Look out for a white painted milestone. This is a milestone with a difference because it indicates the way to Ulverston via the over-sands route.

4. Turn left at the milestone and follow another minor road to the Pig and Whistle. Bear left and continue for about a mile along a minor road with wonderful views of fields and woodlands to left and right.

5. Turn right onto a wide track leading to a dwelling called Longlands. Bear left and then sharp right along field paths and passing a disused quarry on the left. The route now climbs steeply to reach a tower called the Hospice.

The Hospice stands atop Hampsfield Fell which is an area of unspoiled limestone pavement which is much loved by botanists. The Hospice is not a monastic building but a Victorian folly constructed by a Mr Remington in 1846 as a shelter for walkers. We strollers are still grateful for his gift. Climb the steps to the top and, on a clear day, you can almost see forever.

The gatehouse protected the Priory at Cartmel from invading Scots.

Look for the Lake District mountains, the sea sweeping into Morecambe Bay and the three peaks of Ingleborough, Whernside and Penyghent which dominate the Yorkshire Dales.

6. From the Hospice, descend the steep, well-marked track. Pass Pit Farm on the left.

This path is marked on the OS map as Cistercian Way, which is somewhat misleading since the Cartmel monks were Augustinians. Many years ago the local folk referred to this route as the Monks Track, which is certainly more accurate.

7. The path now approaches a set of stone steps. Descend the steps to a narrow road. About 30 yards to the left find another narrow road; turn right and continue to Wheelhouse Bridge. There was once a monastic corn mill situated at this point. The house remains, but the old wheel has gone. From the bridge bear left and return to the Priory gatehouse and then to the car park.

Walk 20
ULVERSTON

Here is a walk of great variety. There are sea views, a stroll along a canal towpath, and a climb up to a lighthouse from which there are panoramic views over Morecambe Bay. Here too are connections with 'Mutiny on the Bounty' and with Stan Laurel. This is a gentle route and is not 'hardy' and is easy to follow and therefore no stroller will ever find themselves in 'another fine mess'.

The Lighthouse Tea and Coffee Shop and Restaurant is open daily from 9.30 am to 5 pm. It is adjacent to the Booths Supermarket, and is part of the Cumbria Crystal and Heron Glass complex, which includes a shop and an opportunity to watch glass-blowers at work. A display area features the work of the comedy duo *Laurel and Hardy* and the history of the monument perched on top of Hoad Hill, built in the style of the former Eddystone lighthouse.

All-day breakfasts are a feature of the teashop as are the Lakeland cream teas. There is a take-away service, which, since the teashop is at the half-way point of the walk, is particularly convenient if you want to enjoy a

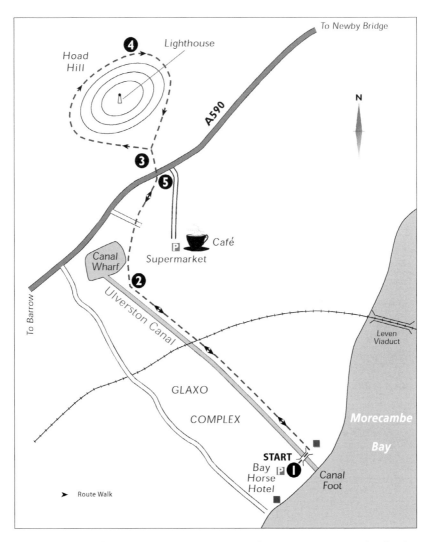

picnic on one of the benches set around the footpath up to Hoad Hill. The café is 'dog friendly' and there are water bowls provided for them. Telephone: 01229 581121.

DISTANCE: 3½ miles
TIME: Allow 2½ hours
MAP: OS Explorer OL 6
STARTING POINT: The (free) car park at Canal Foot (GR 313775).

94

HOW TO GET THERE: From the M6 turn off at Junction 36 and follow the A591 and then the A590(T) to Ulverston. At the entrance to Ulverston approach a roundabout with Booths supermarket to the left. Continue along the A590 for about 200 yards and then turn left along a very minor road signed Canal Foot. Continue on this road for around a mile passing an industrial area on the left (which is dominated by Glaxo Smith Kline pharmaceutical works). At the end of this road are Canal Foot and the coastline with the car park on the left. To the right is the Bay Horse Inn.

THE WALK

The Bay Horse (telephone 01229 583972) is a fascinating hostelry with the famous chef John Tovey as its chairman. Its history dates back at least to 1781 when coaches waited for the tide timings to be right for the crossing of the sands to Lancaster. And, for rail enthusiasts, this is the place to watch rail traffic passing over the viaduct on its way to and from Ulverston.

1. Follow the towpath along the entire length of Ulverston Canal to reach the canal basin.

The canal was completed in the 1790s and was the shortest, straightest and deepest canal to be built in Britain – it is one mile long, 65 feet wide and 15 feet deep. The canal was closed to commercial traffic in 1916 but, in its heyday, it was very busy and Ulverston became prosperous in consequence.

2. At the end of the basin turn right to the A590. To the right is the supermarket and the Lighthouse Tea Shop. Continue on the pavement beside the A590 for about 300 yards until a footpath to the left indicates Hoad Hill. (The A590 is busy but there are three crossing points.)

3. Turn sharp right on this footpath and make your way along the steep and winding track to the top. There are plenty of well-placed seats here where you can make the most of the wonderful views.

Ulverston is proud to lay claim to two famous sons. Sir John Barrow was born in 1764. He was a geographer and travelled to remote places drawing maps. He gave his name to Barrow Strait, Barrow Sound and Barrow Point in the Arctic and Cape Barrow in the Antarctic, and the duck, Barrow's Goldeneye, is named after him. He rose to become

Canal Foot, with the Bay Horse to the right.

Second Secretary to the Admiralty and it was he who wrote the official account of the Mutiny on the Bounty, published in 1831.

Stan Laurel (1890–1965) was born in Ulverston, and his partnership with Oliver Hardy was one of the most successful comedy duos of all time.

On the summit of the 595 ft Hoad Hill stands a monument built in 1850 to commemorate the life of Sir John Barrow. It is a replica of the first Eddystone lighthouse, and inside are stone steps leading to the top of the monument which is occasionally open to the public. Even if the lighthouse is not open, the amazing views from the top of the hill are worth the effort.

4. Follow the track as it winds to the right and descends steeply.

☕ **5.** As the route crosses the A590, turn right and reach the Lighthouse Teashop on the left. Continue for 200 yards and you will find the sign for the canal. Turn left beside it and return to Canal Foot along the towpath.